Barnyard Buddies

In the Turkey Pen

by Patricia M. Stockland
illustrated by Todd Ouren

Special thanks to content consultant:
James S. Cullor, DVM, PhD

magic wagon

visit us at www.abdopublishing.com

Published by Magic Wagon, a division of the ABDO Group, 8000 West 78th Street, Edina, Minnesota 55439. Copyright © 2010 by Abdo Consulting Group, Inc. International copyrights reserved in all countries. All rights reserved. No part of this book may be reproduced in any form without written permission from the publisher.

Looking Glass Library™ is a trademark and logo of Magic Wagon.

Printed in the United States.

♻ Manufactured with paper containing at least 10% post-consumer waste

Text by Patricia M. Stockland
Illustrations by Todd Ouren
Edited by Amy Van Zee
Interior layout and design by Becky Daum
Cover design by Becky Daum

Library of Congress Cataloging-in-Publication Data
Stockland, Patricia M.
  In the turkey pen / by Patricia M. Stockland ; illustrated by Todd Ouren.
    p. cm. — (Barnyard buddies)
  Includes index.
  ISBN 978-1-60270-646-0
  1. Turkeys—Juvenile literature. I. Ouren, Todd, ill. II. Title.
  SF507.S76 2010
  636.5'92—dc22

2009007491

The hens rustle their feathers as they brood over their eggs. **Gobble, gobble, gobble.** The turkeys start their day.

A hen is a female turkey. Brooding is when a hen covers her eggs to keep them warm.

Some poults have just hatched. They are covered in soft down.

Baby turkeys are called poults.

The poults will stay in the brooding area for a while. During their first few weeks, poults need to be kept very warm.

Farmers use heat lamps and clean bedding to keep brooding pens warm, clean, and dry.

The poults eat ground grains. The farmer brings fresh food and water every day.

Turkeys eat corn, oats, and other grains and grasses. They also like insects.

As the poults grow, their feathers fill in. They are no longer covered in down. Now, they are big enough to go outside.

Turkeys take dust baths to get bugs off their feathers.
A turkey rolls on the ground to cover its entire body in dust.
It even uses its wings to scoop dust onto its head and sides. 11

The farmer moves the young turkeys to an outdoor pen. The turkeys peck the ground for yummy insects.

Turkeys eat sand and gravel. Inside their bodies, the sand and gravel help mash the turkeys' food.

The turkeys enjoy their feed. Then, they fan their feathers. They perch on roosts.

When turkeys get strong enough, they rest on roosts, or large branches.

When the turkeys are six months old, they are full sized. The farmer takes some of the grown turkeys to market. Other turkeys stay on the farm.

Turkeys are raised for meat, feathers, and for showing.

The farmer takes the biggest and best turkeys to the fair. The turkeys are judged. Some are given ribbons.

At fairs, turkeys are judged on their health, size, and appearance.

When the turkeys get home, they settle back in their pen. The hens sit on their roosts. Next spring, they will have their own poults.

Gobble, gobble, gobble!

21

Turkey Diagram

fanned tail feathers

eye

beak

wattle

wing

claw

Glossary

down—tiny, soft feathers that keep a bird warm.

grains—feed such as corn and oats.

hatch—to come out of an egg.

heat lamps—lights used by farmers to keep young birds and other animals warm.

market—where animals are bought and sold.

perch—to rest or balance on a branch.

Fun Facts

Wild turkeys are darker and have smaller, leaner bodies than turkeys on farms. They also have bright pink legs. Wild turkeys can fly, and they like to roost in trees.

Hens do not gobble as loudly as male turkeys do. Hens make quieter clicking sounds.

Turkeys do not chew their food. Instead, the sand and gravel they swallow help crush foods in the gizzard. This helps the turkey digest its food.

The turkey was almost the national bird of the United States. Benjamin Franklin suggested it.

Some birds and other animals cannot see in color, but turkeys can. Turkeys also hear very well.

Most large modern turkey farms do not hatch their own eggs. Instead, they order young poults from other farms, called hatcheries.

Turkeys roll in the dust to clean themselves of any bugs. The bugs can't breathe through the coating of dust, so they fall off.

Index

bedding 7

brooding 3, 6

dust baths 11

eggs 3

fairs 18, 19

farmer 7, 8, 12, 16, 18

feathers 3, 4, 10, 11, 14, 17

food 8, 9, 12, 13, 14

heat lamps 7

hen 3, 20

market 16

pens 7, 12, 20

poults 4, 5, 6, 8, 10, 20

roosts 14, 15, 20